Old Navajo Rugs

Old Navajo Rugs

Their Development From 1900 to 1940

Marian E. Rodee

University of New Mexico Press
Albuquerque

Library of Congress Cataloging in Publication Data

Rodee, Marian E.
  Old Navajo rugs.

  Bibliography: p.
  Includes index.
  1. Navaho Indians—Rugs.   2. Indians of North America—Southwest, New—
Rugs.   I. Title.
E99.N3R59   746.7′2   80-54560
ISBN 0-8263-0566-0   AACR2
ISBN 0-8263-0567-9 (pbk.)

International Standard Book Number (clothbound)
0-8263-0566-0

International Standard Book Number (paperbound)
0-8263-0567-9

Sixth paperbound printing 1989

For Kathy and Susie

Contents

List of Illustrations

Plates

Figures

List of Illustrations

Acknowledgments

My special thanks go to the National Endowment for the Arts for giving me the initial time to start the research on this project under a Fellowship for Museum Professionals. Of course, the research took longer than I had planned, and thanks are due to J. J. Brody, Director of the Maxwell Museum, for allowing me time to finish the manuscript.

The real effort was expended by my colleagues at other museums who helped me locate and haul out thousands of pounds of Navajo weaving: Marcia Gallagher, Museum of Northern Arizona; Susan McGreevy, Wheelwright Museum; H. Thomas Cain, Heard Museum; U. Vincent Wilcox, Museum of the American Indian; Dee Ulrich, Southwest Museum; Jan Bell, Arizona State Museum; Claudia Medoff, University of Pennsylvania Museum; Jan Timbrook, Santa Barbara Museum of Natural History; Nancy Blomberg, Los Angeles County Museum of Natural History; Stovall Museum, University of Oklahoma; and Kent Bush and Liz Bauer, Hubbell Trading Post National Historic Site.

Preface

Old Navajo rugs exert an appeal that is frequently lacking in contemporary weaving. In contrast with many modern rugs that are sold as wall hangings, beautiful but remote from their original function, old Navajo rugs remain engaging, well woven, strong. This book is designed to fill a lacuna in their history—the period from 1890 to World War II. I hope, thereby, to assist both private and public collectors who are turning to this period as nineteenth-century weaving becomes increasingly expensive.

With the aid of 77 photographs and plates, I show how and why Navajo rugs woven during these fifty years differ from those produced in earlier and later periods. For though the dissimilarities between Classic blankets and Eyedazzlers and early rugs are quite striking, the variations between early and late rugs are more subtle.

I began my research by traveling around the country to explore the wealth of rugs in public collections. I examined thousands of rugs and collected data on about 700 pieces. The museums I visited rarely had much information about these items, for old rugs were often curios, souvenirs from a patron's trip west. Of the rugs I examined, for example, only one or two were identified by the Navajo weaver's name, and only about 150 were really well dated. But even knowing the exact date of purchase does not establish when a rug was woven, for it is quite probable that the trader/seller had the rug for several years before its sale.

Further limitations to dating these weavings become apparent. Before World War II, for instance, many of the remote areas of the Navajo Reservation were inaccessible. Furthermore, in many cases, although we may be able to pin down the date a pattern began, we may not be able to tell when it ended, for once a design enters the repertory of Navajo weaving it continues to be used again and again. To complicate matters even more, we must understand how the wishes and preferences of a trader or customer may very well influence style.

This is to say, then, that the statements in this book should not be considered absolute, but rather only generally true for a certain area or time. I do not believe, however, that more precise detail will ever be possible.

1

Navajo Weaving Before 1890

Navajo women have been excellent weavers for at least the past three hundred years, perhaps even before the Reconquest of New Mexico in 1692. It was then that the Spanish army, led by Don Diego de Vargas, ended the Pueblo Rebellion of 1680 in which the Spanish settlers were driven out of the territory. Fearing reprisals by the returning conquistadors, many Pueblo families took shelter among the Navajo—even though the groups had never been on the best of terms because of the frequent raids by the seminomadic and warlike Navajo upon the crops and livestock of their more peaceful settled neighbors. Nevertheless, it is probably from these Pueblo refugees that the Navajos learned to weave.

Although the Navajo knew and used cotton, as did prehistoric Indians in the Southwest long before them, it was wool from sheep introduced by the Spanish that would become their most important textile fiber. By the early eighteenth century, the Navajo were described by Spanish writers as being fine weavers; a hundred years later, in 1812, they were called the best weavers in the province (Pedro Piño, *Exposición de Nuevo Mexico*, 1812). The few extant textiles that date from the eighteenth century are archaeological finds.

But it is with the discovery of the cache from Massacre

Cave at Canyon de Chelly, Arizona, that our knowledge of Navajo weaving really begins. In 1804, in this cave, a group of Navajo took cover from Spanish soldiers on a retaliatory mission against an Indian raiding party. When the last soldier had passed the hiding place, one of the Indians let out a victory cry, whereupon the soldiers turned and fired. Their bullets struck the cave overhang and ricocheted into the shelter, killing all the people within.

Because of the Navajo fear of the dead, Massacre Cave remained undisturbed for a hundred years until Sam Day, a local trader, entered it and brought to light the weaving that had lain untouched. The store of textiles he found, broke up, and sold to museums throughout the country included, among the many woven of plain stripes, some that showed the beginnings of more elaborate patterns of terraces and diamonds.

With the opening of the Santa Fe Trail in 1822 and the ensuing greatly expanded eastern trade with the Southwest, Navajo weaving becomes common enough to study. In what is generally known as the Classic period—prior to 1880—we find that the textiles were all *blankets*, used as saddle blankets, or worn as dresses by the women and as outer garments by both sexes of all ages. So finely woven were these blankets that they became a valuable trade item with other tribes, sometimes reaching groups as far away from Navajo country as the Sioux of the Dakotas. Soldiers and ranchers prized these textiles as warm and watertight bedding. Indeed, in 1850 a Navajo blanket was so highly valued that it was priced at fifty dollars in gold, a very considerable sum at that time.

When we attempt to identify and date blankets of the Classic period, we find ourselves looking closely at pattern, of course. We discover that in Classic weaving the patterns are primarily banded, usually of five separate units (Plate 1). One theory is that the Navajo developed their more complex patterns from rather simple ones, first weaving plain stripes and then going on to arrange the stripes in groups, eventually adding extra design motifs such as zigzags, wavy lines, and diamonds, as we see here. But we should bear in mind that Navajo weaving tends to be rather conservative, and although a pattern sometimes seems to disappear, it may very well reappear over the generations. Plain stripes, for example, have never been entirely abandoned; they have always been a major element in Navajo design.

Even if pattern and design changes are, at first glance, the most obvious keys to weaving identification, more significant clues beyond the passage of time and the vagaries of style are to be found by examining the materials each weaver used. These, more than patterns, are the best dating tools for the collector. We must attend to the qualities of fiber and dye, and ask ourselves specifically: is the material handspun and hand-dyed? or is it commercial yarn, fibers spun by machine in a mill and dyed in large lots? and what is the ply, the number of individual strands twisted together?

Classic period weaving, most popularly a red, white, and blue combination, frequently contains a three-ply vegetal-dyed yarn called *Saxony*. Originally a reference to a breed of sheep developed in Saxony, Germany, the term has come to designate all high quality, natural-dyed, silky yarns. The red was either Saxony yarn or raveled trade cloth called *bayeta*, Spanish for baize, a plain wool cloth manufactured in England. Since red was the most difficult color to obtain from desert Southwest dyes, red cloth was the most commonly raveled, though other colors, especially green, are known to have been raveled as well. The original dye is cochineal, extracted from a beetle parasite of the nopal cactus of Mexico and Central America. A long path—from Mexico to Spain to England to the Navajo of the New World!

Since plants of the southwestern deserts usually yield dyes of yellow and green, blue was also difficult to obtain. Therefore, indigo was brought in to provide a range of shades from near black to light blue. Purchased in lumps, it was used by the Indians with their handspun wool. And when mixed with yellow from an indigenous plant like rabbit brush, for example, it produced a rich, clear green.

(Black, by the way, was obtained by dyeing naturally dark wool with a concoction of piñon pitch and ashes.)

So there we have it, the spectrum to look for in Classic period blankets—red, white, blue, black, locally dyed green and yellow, and natural gray, beige, and carded pink—the palette of the Navajo weaver before 1880.

Possibly as a result of the confinement of the Navajo at Bosque Redondo and their exposure to outside influences in the 1860s, an increasing complexity in Classic design becomes apparent around 1870. The Navajo were interned at Bosque Redondo by the United States army in 1864 in a federal government attempt to change their traditional life-style of herding and raiding by settling them in a new area to learn farming. As prisoners and wards of the government, they were deprived of their livestock and were issued non-Navajo supplies and clothing, including Saltillo blankets from northern Mexico (Wheat 1976:432). As a result of their close confinement with the soldiers and their families, the Navajo were exposed to many new concepts. Navajo women responded by evolving a dress style of long flounced calico skirts and velvet blouses with collars, a fashion still observed today. During the 1870s, Classic weaving patterns become increasingly vertical, that is, running up and down the blanket rather than in horizontal bands. The small zigzags of the Saltillo blanket are blown up into large motifs.

After their release from Bosque Redondo in 1869 and after their return to their old territories now established as a Reservation, the Navajo received traders licensed by the government. Soon, flour, coffee, tools, and other materials necessary to their new life poured in. When the railroad came through the southern edge of the Navajo Reservation in 1880 and 1881, an even greater flood of manufactured goods became available. It wasn't long before Navajo women realized how much easier it would be to buy ready-made Pendleton blankets than to weave their traditional garments.

But the railroad also brought new weaving supplies in the form of new dyes and yarns. In contrast to the vegetal dyes of the Classic period, these were anilines derived from coal tar. The color combinations now possible were extremely gaudy—red, orange, green, purple, and yellow, often woven next to one another in the same blanket. This profusion of color led the old traders and writers to coin the derogatory term "eyedazzler"—a word that has lasted to characterize this period (Plate 2). However, tastes have changed dramatically since then, and weaving dated between 1880 and the turn of the century has become increasingly popular with collectors.

With the Eyedazzler period emerge some interesting new developments in the evolution of Navajo weaving, short cuts in the weaving process, if you will. In addition to aniline dyes sold in little packets for use by weavers on their own handspun wool, four-ply aniline-dyed yarn came to the Reservation. Called Germantown yarn, for the Pennsylvania town where it was manufactured, it was fairly expensive and came into the hands of only the best weavers. Consequently, Germantown yarn rugs are invariably finely woven.

Some collectors decry the Eyedazzler period as "degenerate" because of the use of predyed and spun yarn and even cotton string warp (ordinary package twine from the trading post that was not as strong as handspun wool), and because of what they see as the abandonment of traditional weaving skills. And it is true that during this period a weaver could make a blanket without the labor of shearing, carding, spinning, and dyeing her wool first. It follows, however, that these ready-made materials freed her to spend more time at her loom working at elaborate and intricately woven patterns. Indeed, a survey of the Eyedazzler period reveals it to be, after all, one of great imagination and creativity in design and explosions of color.

The railroad that brought the new materials which would change the face of weaving styles, also brought the manufactured fabrics that signaled the demise of the traditional blanket. But the traders to the Reservation realized how important weaving was to the Navajo economy—and by extension, of course, to their own—and sought new outlets for the new textiles. So, gradually, the weavers turned from making exceptionally fine blankets for their own use and trade to weaving rugs for the floors of Anglo buyers. They adapted their choice of materials accordingly: the textiles became larger, heavier, generally coarser, frequently marked by a border of stripes or a stepped fret. A photograph dated as early as 1871 shows a weaver at a loom weaving a piece with a stepped border. In time, the pattern of framelike border around a central design would emerge to replace the earlier style of horizontal bands. However, it would take many years for the new look to predominate. Clearly, from the time the traders moved into Navajo country, the history of rug weaving reflects a succession of their efforts to improve the quality of Navajo rugs and make them more marketable.

2

The Transitional Period, 1890 to 1920

Earlier writers on the subject of Navajo weaving have called the period from 1880 to 1900 "transitional," for it saw the introduction of new color patterns and styles. I would like to extend the use of this term to the period from 1890 to 1920, for at this time traders were introducing even more radically different designs that owed little to Navajo traditions. Collectors who wish to date and identify weaving from this period must keep in mind the trends that were emerging toward subtler designs and heavier, coarser fabric, as the era of the Navajo blanket passed and the age of the Navajo rug became established.

One of the most common design layouts we find at this time is a bold horizontal banded pattern, a rather coarsened version of the Classic blanket, with one or two stripes across the top and bottom (Plate 3). If we had no early photographic evidence of complete borders on rugs of the 1870s, how easily we might mistake these simple stripes for the first steps in the development of the bordered rug.

During the 1890s, Navajo weavers continued to draw on raveled material for their fiber, now aniline-dyed trade cloth, not cochineal. And although they still used indigo until the turn of the century, they looked to it less and less as aniline blue increased in popularity. The consequences of this become apparent with the passage of time, and afford additional keys to identification for the collector. Probably the finest natural dye in the world, renowned since antiquity, indigo remains rich and stable for centuries; on the other hand, in less than a hundred years most aniline blues become gray purples.

Perhaps one of the more striking characteristics of the Transitional period is the reaction that occurred against the color riot of the earlier Eyedazzlers, and the turning to subtler, quieter shades more suitable to the floors of parlors. The Navajo weaver of this period worked with a palette of fewer colors, orange, red, black, and white being the most popular combination. Even the weavers who continued to make Eyedazzlers tended to rely on a narrower range than the spectrum of the 1880s.

At the same time as a subdued blanket style became popular in the 1890s, a new rug style was arising. The colors were somber—gray, black, or white backgrounds —with large, bold figures in red, black, and gray floating against the ground. (See Plates 4 and 5 for typical examples of color and pattern.) Note that the large, simple figures no longer have outlines, serrations, or other blanket refinements. It is this style that will prevail over the more traditional blanket, and be found all over the Reservation from the mid-1890s to 1915, gradually disappearing as individual traders encouraged more distinctive, technically superior styles.

In response to the growing demand for rugs, the format of Navajo weaving also adapted. Traditional blankets had been woven in more or less standard sizes: single saddle, double saddle or children's, men's, women's, and chief's (the latter two types woven wider than long). The most common size became the four-by-six-foot rug or blanket which is probably a larger version of the men's blanket, just as the three-by-five-foot rug is a slightly larger form of the thirty-by-sixty-inch double saddle blanket. As Navajo weaving became more widely known and the market increased, many very large rugs were produced to order for specific rooms, including runners for hallways and front porches, and even pairs of rugs for adjoining rooms.

Very often it is difficult to distinguish blankets of the 1890s from rugs of the same period, especially if they have been woven from handspun yarns. It becomes largely a matter of personal opinion whether a weaving is light-weight enough to wear. In contrast, Germantown textiles are always relatively fine and light, even when their size and pattern clearly mark them as rugs.

Quality of wool, in effect, offers some of the best clues to identifying pieces from the Transitional period. Textiles from these years are frequently called *pound rugs* because of the traders' practice of paying for them by weight, under the mistaken assumption that this would encourage the weavers to produce more. That is not what happened. Instead, the Navajo women outsmarted the traders by weaving loose, coarse rugs from poorly cleaned and carded wool and then pounding more dirt and sand into the finished product. This increased the weight of the rug, but did nothing to enhance the quality.

Other factors may have contributed to the general coarseness of Transitional period textiles, including a decline in the craft of spinning as a result of the introduction of so much commercial yarn, to say nothing of the varying qualities of wool available as the native Navajo sheep changed. This question, and the significance of the quality and identification of fiber to rug dating in general, will be thoroughly discussed next.

3

Fiber:
The Key to Identification

As we turn our attention to the heart of this book—Navajo weaving from 1900 to 1940—we must reiterate that the single most important criterion for dating these pieces is wool type and quality. We have suggested earlier that the historical patterns of Navajo weaving are interesting, valuable sources for tracing and identifying specific textiles. But establishing the pattern of a rug does not guarantee an accurate dating. We may observe many examples today of patterns that have been revived or just continued in the hands of a conservative weaver. Styles that date from the early to mid-nineteenth century, like striped and banded blankets, and the famous chief's blanket, are still being woven. Given this understanding, what is the buyer and collector to do? Learn as much as possible about pattern, looms, and traditional weaving techniques, of course. But most of all, study and become familiar with the raw fiber itself. To this end the following pages are dedicated.

Domestic sheep have fleeces made up of three types of fiber: a true wool, constituting the shorter inner coat; kemp, a long coarse outer fiber with a large medulla (central core); and hair, an intermediate fiber with a large medulla in the summer and a small one in winter. The proportion of these fibers in a fleece determines the quality

11

of the handspun wool. The more fine, true wool, the better the fleece. The more kemp, the coarser the yarn, since a large medulla means a coarse and brittle fiber. Furthermore, the fineness of the short wool fibers, expressed by the average diameter of the strands, and the amount of crimp or curl are also important. Tight curly wool is more difficult to handspin than long straight fibers.

This brings us to the question of the type of sheep the Navajo first acquired. For the answer, we must go to Spain.

The general purposes of sheep breeding have been to produce an animal suitable to a particular locale, type of range, fodder, or textile industry. In Spain, two groups of sheep developed, the *Estantes*, or "stationary" kind, and the *Transhumantes*, or "migrating" variety. The *churro*, one of the Estante breed, was well suited to sparse lowland country. The *merino*, in contrast, was one of the finest sheep in the world, bred and improved by the Spanish from a breed common throughout the Mediterranean regions of the Roman Empire. The pampered merinos were pastured all over the country, driven across the lands and crops of the common people, into the mountains in summer, down to the plains in winter, because of the incorrect belief that this change improved the wool. These merino flocks, the property of the royal family and the nobility, were bred just for the fine, short-stapled quality of their wool, not for adaptation to a special range. The Spanish textile industry flourished because of them. They were so prized that the crime of exporting them from Spain was punishable by death.

The sheep brought by the Spanish to the New World, then, were almost certainly churros, not merinos, although the churros probably had a great deal of merino blood. Churros were perfectly suited to the Southwest, which had a climate similar to Spain. Their relatively fine, long-stapled wool was also well suited to the Navajo handspindle.

The Navajo initially accumulated their flocks by trade or raids on Spanish ranches and Pueblo Indian farms. However, at the time of their forced relocation and containment at Bosque Redondo in the 1860s, their live-stock was seized. In 1869, when their chiefs signed a peace treaty that allowed them to return to their former lands, they were allotted $30,000 by the federal government to reestablish their flocks of sheep and goats. With this sum the Navajo purchased fourteen thousand sheep and a thousand goats from the Luceros ranch near Mora, New Mexico (Underhill 1953:190). That these sheep were un-doubtedly churros is borne out by examination of the wool in blankets woven before and after Bosque Redondo. (This information is different from Charles A. Amsden's in his classic book, *Navaho Weaving* [1934]. Based on the word of an old trader who remembered reading it in a newspaper, Amsden reports that the Navajo were supplied with American crossbreds.)

The new peace treaty after Bosque Redondo forbade Navajo forays against their neighbors; hence, they were limited to crossbreeding within their own flocks. Although the number of animals increased, through indiscriminate breeding the quality of wool declined. From the 1870s to the 1890s, as an examination of surviving blankets shows, Navajo wool gradually coarsened. We see more long kemp fibers and less fine wool. This trend reached its lowest point in the 1890s, and, as we have already noted, gave rugs of this transitional decade a very heavy, coarse appearance. Sometimes we find a rug that has received so little wear and has such long kemp fibers that it appears to have a pile (Figure 1). Usually, however, with any wear at all, the brittle kemp breaks off.

By the turn of the century, federal agents realized the need to improve the Navajo flocks, and in 1903 Rambouil-let rams were introduced (Underhill 1953:236). These sheep were descendents of the flock of merinos given by the Spanish crown during the eighteenth century to Louis XV of France who crossbred them with French sheep at the royal estate at Rambouillet. When they were finally imported by American sheepmen, the Rambouillet became very popular, especially in New England, for they produced good meat and a heavy fleece. Around 1920 they

Figure 1. Detail of a Transitional period rug, c. 1900, showing long kemp fibers. Private collection. Michael Mouchette, photographer.

were bred so extensively with Navajo sheep (Grandstaff 1942:4) that between 1920 and 1940 their wool predominated.

The large-bodied French breed adapted very well to the rugged terrain of the Navajo Reservation, but their fleece was not well suited to the needs of Navajo weaving. First of all, it was greasy, and had to be well washed to take dyes, frequently a difficult step considering the general scarcity of water on the Reservation. By comparison, churro wool produced much less natural grease. To complicate matters, Rambouillet is a very short-stapled wool with a tight crimp, properties that, as we have noted, make it difficult to hand spin. Therefore, we find that rugs woven between 1920 and 1940 have a distinctive curly wool. Very bad examples look

14   Chapter 3

knotted and lumpy. It is this characteristic that makes examples from this period so easy to identify.

Let's take an example, and compare two rugs as shown in Plates 6a through 7b. In Plate 6a, we see a rug of the 1890s with a dominant zigzag pattern, a traditional motif expanded to cover the whole textile. Plate 6b shows a rug with the same pattern that was woven during the two decades we are discussing. In these pieces, we may observe some characteristic changes: the 1890s rug still has some bright Eyedazzler colors, while the newer rug, demonstrating the persistence of an old design, is made up of a simple black, white, red, and beige combination bordered on four sides. The details of both rugs, as seen in Plate 7, illustrate a more subtle distinction, the point we have been making about the quality of wool. The older rug exhibits the coarse kempy wool we may expect of the Transitional period: the wool is straight and thick, and would have resembled the detail in Figure 1 before the long fibers wore off. Indeed, if you look down into the wefts you can see the ends of the remaining kemp. In contrast, Plate 7b shows the tight kinky twist of later period Rambouillet.

In an effort to solve some of the problems posed by the Rambouillet, the U.S. Department of the Interior and the Department of Agriculture established the Southwestern Range and Sheep Breeding Laboratory at Fort Wingate, New Mexico, in 1935. The aim of the program was to develop a breed of sheep whose wool was similar to the nineteenth-century strain, yet would provide adequate meat. The Fort Wingate scientists began their research by acquiring all the old churro sheep they could, usually finding them in remote areas of the Reservation. They even employed a Navajo weaver to test the wool resulting from their experiments. The new types of sheep were then successfully crossbred with the old Navajo sheep, and the offspring were distributed to the Indians.

The work of the Sheep Breeding Laboratory was greatly curtailed by World War II when Fort Wingate was again used for military purposes. As a result, we may say that the age of Rambouillet wool in Navajo weaving lasted from

1920 to 1940. Since then, Navajo wool has resumed its original appearance (Figure 2). However, Rambouillet sheep continued to supply the brown and gray wool used by weavers, so it is best to examine the white and dyed yarns to determine the age.

Some technical points that would be helpful in identifying weaving from this period are probably well worth mentioning here. Generally the proportion of wefts to warps is five to one, rather than the lower count of the Transitional period or the finer count of the Classics and Germantowns. Warps are almost always white handspun wool, rather than the cotton string or the sometimes colored handspun of the Classic period. Edge cords are never jarring or unusual, but usually a harmonious black, white, or gray. The dyes are normally aniline. Black, white, red, beige, and gray are the standard colors. These may include

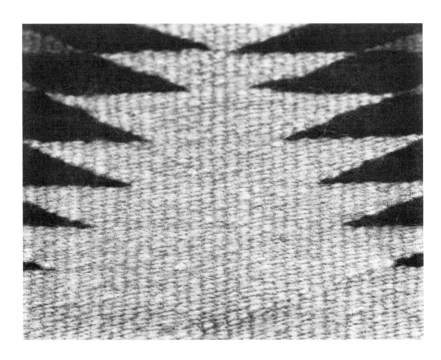

Figure 2. Detail of rug woven at the Fort Wingate School with newly developed wool (1944). Maxwell Museum, University of New Mexico. Jim Bechdel, photographer.

a pleasant camel shade, which in many rugs is a natural sheep wool, but was also often imitated by either a vegetal or aniline dye. (See Plate 6b).

My personal observations of the differences in wool types during the course of this study have been reinforced by the papers and the wool samples deposited by the Fort Wingate Experimental Station with the Wheelwright Museum, and by the published results of the experiments at Fort Wingate by James O. Grandstaff (Technical Bulletin No. 790, January 1942).

Plate 1. Classic period wearing blanket, c. 1870–80. Maxwell Museum of Anthropology, University of New Mexico. Bruce Moore, photographer.

Plate 2. Eyedazzler blanket in Germantown yarn, c. 1880–90.
Private collection. Bruce Moore, photographer.

Plate 3.   Late nineteenth-century blanket of handspun yarn, c. 1890–1900. Private collection. Bruce Moore, photographer.

Plate 4. Transitional period rug, c. 1900–1915. Private collection. Bruce Moore, photographer.

Plate 5.   Transitional period rug, c. 1900–1915. Private collection. Bruce Moore, photographer.

Plate 6a. Transitional period rug, c. 1890–1910. James Brecher collection. Bruce Moore, photographer.

Plate 6b. Rug, 1920–40. Private collection. Michael Mouchette, photographer.

Plate 7a. Detail of 6a. Michael Mouchette, photographer.

Plate 7b. Detail of 6b. Michael Mouchette, photographer.

Plate 8.   Rug bought in 1915 at Crystal, New Mexico. Maxwell
Museum of Anthropology, University of New Mexico.

Plate 9. Two Grey Hills rug purchased at Newcomb, New Mexico in 1929. Arizona State Museum, University of Arizona, Tucson.

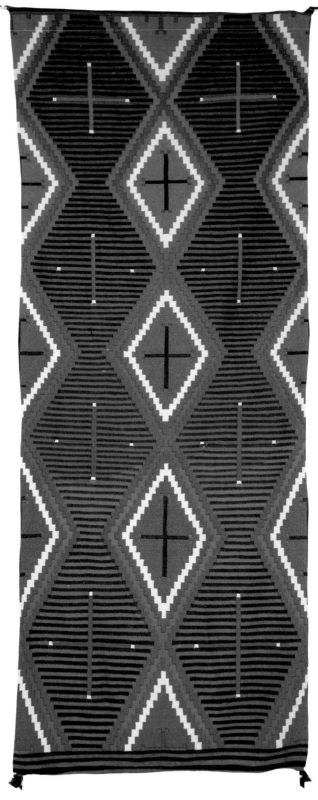

Plate 10.   Hubbell Moki Revival rug, c. 1890–1910. Private collection. Bruce Moore, photographer.

a.

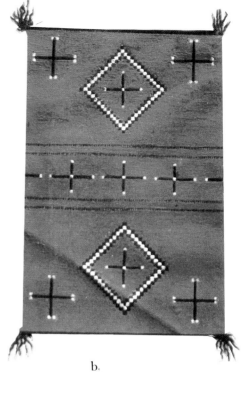

b.

Plate 11(a-d). Four paintings of blanket patterns at Hubbell Trading Post National Historic Site. Kent Bush, photographer.

d.

c.

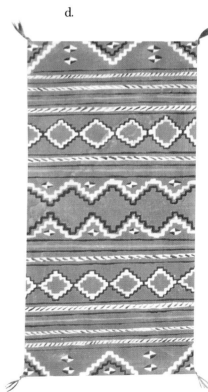

a.

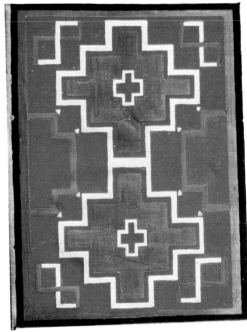

b.

Plate 12(a-d). Four paintings of rug styles at Hubbell Trading Post National Historic Site. Kent Bush, photographer.

c.

d.

Plate 13. Ganado rug, 1920–40. Private collection. Michael Mouchette, photographer.

Plate 14. Revival style rug woven in 1930s at Fort Wingate School with vegetal and chrome dyes. Wheelwright Museum, Santa Fe.

Plate 15.   Mountain. Chant sandpainting rug, woven in 1936 by
Hosteen Klah. Private collection. Bruce Moore, photographer.

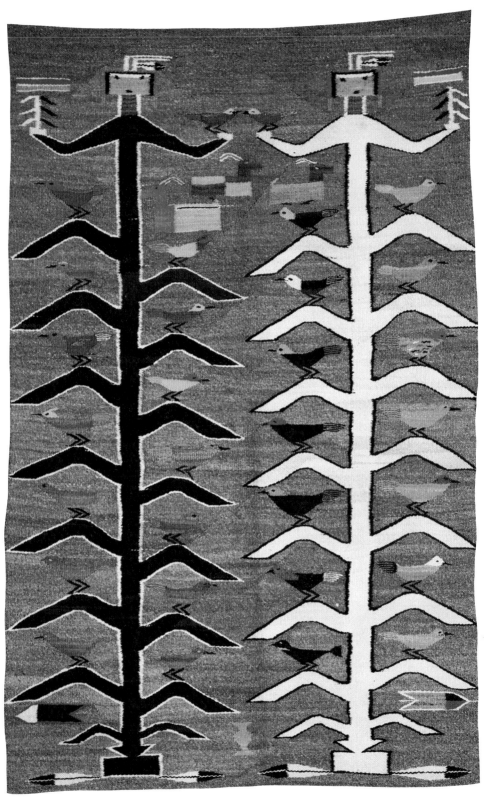

Plate 16. Pictorial rug, Corn People, 1920–40. Private collection. Michael Mouchette, photographer.

4

J. B. Moore and the Crystal Trading Post

In 1897, J. B. Moore bought the trading post at Washington Pass in the Chuska Mountains of New Mexico, and renamed it Crystal for the clear spring that flowed nearby. The post had been built by Joe Wilkin in 1894, but neither he nor subsequent traders had fared well there. Although John Moore was in business only until 1911, he played a great role in influencing Navajo weaving in his area.

For one thing, Moore tried to improve the quality of wool used in his rugs by having it cleaned and dyed under his wife's supervision. For even finer grades of rugs, he sent some wool to a commercial scouring plant for preparation. He limited the colors of his rugs to black white, gray, red, and blue, a far more subtle range than the Eyedazzlers, and he proudly announced in his catalogs that he did not permit the use of Germantown yarns.

Of far greater importance, Moore worked with his weavers for the improvement of rug design, and successfully merchandised their work through a series of advertising leaflets and two illustrated catalogs published in 1903 and 1911. As a result, prospective buyers in other parts of the country could order a rug in the pattern size, and fineness of weave they desired. Plate 8 is an example of a rug ordered from the catalog in 1914 (Figure 22).

Moore was not the first trader to produce an illustrated

catalog of Navajo weaving. That distinction belongs to C. N. Cotton, who left his partnership with Lorenzo Hubbell at Ganado in 1894 to open a wholesale house in Gallup. Cotton began by distributing mimeographed lists of his wares. When this proved successful, he produced a printed catalog showing five rugs (Figures 3 to 7), and announced that although these particular pieces were not for sale—they were representative photographs of the type of rug he handled—similar ones were available through him. Figure 4 is very much like the hooked oriental style that Moore was to popularize.

It would be hard to say which of these important early traders, Cotton, Moore, or Hubbell, invented or originated the patterns advertised during this period. But it would appear that it was Cotton's considerable influence on other traders, who in turn directed their weavers, that brought about the changes in rug patterns in the mid-1890s. In his catalog Cotton explains,

> I decided the only way these people [the Navajo] could prosper, and the traders as well, was to encourage the making of blankets in a commercial way, which I proceeded to do, and by hard and consistent effort I was enabled to sell all I could procure.

After examining the Moore and Cotton catalogs, rug patterns in the trading post at Ganado, and actual rugs dating from 1895 to 1915, I have concluded that there are three basic patterns that mark this period, those based on Classic weaving, the floating style, and the new, dominant, oriental style.

All Moore patterns in the catalogs of 1903 and 1911 are illustrated here, arranged according to style rather than chronology. Only five are reminiscent of blanket patterns of previous periods. Figures 8 and 9 are virtually indistinguishable from blankets with one or two borderlike stripes on the horizontal ends. The pattern of overall interlocking diamonds in Figure 9 is commonly found later, although

not with blanket orientation. Figure 10 shows a straightfor-
ward adaptation of a Classic blanket with horizontal bands,
diamonds, and stripes. An interesting feature here is the
pattern of dashes in contrasting color superimposed on the
basic pattern, very much a Mexican blanket feature. Figure
11 could easily be mistaken for a Hubbell revival piece
with its narrow striped background (see page 66 below).
Although only three patterns have a border of a wavy line
in two colors (Figures 13 through 15), this arrangement
becomes common on rugs for the next forty years.

Among the popular border designs by Moore is the fret,
both plain (Figure 16) and stepped (Figures 17 and 18). This
stepped design is the earliest one used by Navajo weavers,
and has been documented in a photograph of a weaver at
work in 1878. Related to the fret is crenellation, or the
three-stepped type (Figures 19 to 21). Only two (Figures 22
and 23) have stripe borders. Another group consists of
chains or serrated diamonds (Figures 24 to 26) and two in
which the elements have been joined (Figures 27 and 28).
The group represented in Figures 29 to 31 has more
figurative elements—plants, Greek crosses, and what may
be called a tuning fork because of its resemblance to that
object (Figure 29).

We should note that six of the border patterns emphasize
the four corners, a feature that does not persist in Navajo
rugs. And some of these borders, especially the three-
stepped triangle, seem to be based on the patterns in the
older craft of basketry (Figure 32).

Before we examine the central fields of J. B. Moore's rugs,
we should consider the question of the influence of oriental
rugs on Navajo weaving. This was first discussed by Charles
Amsden in 1934, and was explored recently in *East Meets
West*, an exhibit at the Maxwell Museum of the University
of New Mexico. What proofs we have for this influence are
those of logic and visual similarity. For one thing, the very
idea of a bordered floor rug with a central design is
certainly more in keeping with oriental tradition than with
the Navajo. In the late nineteenth and early twentieth

centuries, rugs from the Caucasus—part of present-day Turkey and Russia—were more popular than the flower garden carpets of Iran. It is reasonable to assume that many Anglo families brought such oriental rugs with them when they settled out West. These distinctive patterns also make their appearance just when traders were trying to develop a new market for Navajo weaving beyond the traditional one for the blanket.

Before we discuss the textiles themselves, we should note some similarities between the Navajo and the people of the Caucasus. Both were seminomads who used similar looms and weaving techniques. It is not surprising, then, that similar patterns emerged, for example, the serrated diamonds common to both cultures. Moreover, the bold angular patterns, in both knotted pile and flatly woven techniques, would have been relatively easy for Navajo weavers to understand, interpret, and adapt.

If we compare Figure 26 with Figure 33 we see some striking likenesses. The latter piece belonged to Helen Hunt Jackson, the author of *Ramona*, and is now in the Colorado Springs Pioneers Museum. This rug, from Bergamo, Turkey, incorporates well known Caucasus weaving motifs such as the large central diamond or medallion, either single or double and floating against a plain ground, and the peculiar device resembling an airplane. Figure 19, J. B. Moore's rug, is remarkably similar, a variation of the Bergamo pattern, but on a longer, narrower format.

Looking closely at the details of both rugs, we find that the border of Moore's rug is very much like the Bergamo. Such an unusual motif can not really be attributed to parallel development, but must indicate a deliberate introduction into the Navajo design repertory. Furthermore, an interesting octagonal motif called a *gul* in oriental rug weaving is used in both pieces as a filler. (On oriental rugs it is frequently repeated in rows to form an all over design.) Another prominent oriental feature is the occurrence of spindly hooks protruding from the central medallion (see Figures 23, 25, and 29 especially). These thin hooks also figure in the Bergamo design.

This is not to suggest that J. B. Moore derived the Crystal style totally from the rug owned by Helen Hunt Jackson, but that Caucasus weaving was popular and was being brought out West.

Another explanation for the dissemination of the oriental style can be found in popular items like rug hooking patterns. In the Greenfield Village Henry Ford Museum of Dearborn, Michigan, can be found a set of rug hooking stencils manufactured by the E. S. Frost Co. in the last quarter of the nineteenth century. There are about a dozen of these "Turkish" patterns (Figure 34). Again, this isn't to say that Navajo weavers saw and copied rug hooking designs, but it does prove the widespread popularity of these patterns with Easterners.

Other patterns in the Moore catalog are traditional Navajo designs. Two of the most popular are the Greek cross and the swastika. The former is a cross with arms of equal length that is a popular basketry pattern and the symbol of Spider woman who, according to Navajo teaching, instructed the Navajo people in how to weave (Figure 32). The swastika or "whirling logs" motif comes from sand paintings and is found throughout the Reservation. It is a design element distinctive of the first part of the twentieth century until the late thirties and early forties, when Hitler and the German Nazi Party made the symbol distasteful to Americans.

Motifs that also appear in these rugs are plants (maize) and small birds (Figure 31), as well as the so-called storm, which continues to be woven today (Figure 15). The latter's central square supposedly represents the storm cloud, and the zigzags forming the four corners, lightning. (The curious diamonds with four hooks are called water bugs.) Even after diligent investigation of the sandpaintings, the prototype for the storm pattern is not evident. (It probably continues to be popular because Anglo buyers like to believe that all Native-American art is filled with symbolism.) Both the storm pattern and the blocky diamond (Figure 12) were evidently borrowed from the Western Reservation around Tuba City where they were originated (see Chapter 8). The use of these two borrowed patterns along with a Hubbell revival type indicate that Moore was trying to please all of his customers.

Exactly how all these diverse elements were combined to produce such handsome rugs is still a mystery. Moore claimed that one of his best weavers, Bi-leen Alpai Bi Zha Ahd, devised the patterns (*The Navaho*, 1911). Considering the variety of sophisticated designs in his rugs, this is probably an overstatement, a bit of sales propaganda. As for Moore himself, he was certainly a successful business man and promoter, but I doubt that he, Cotton, or Hubbell had the artistic talent to design such fine, bold rugs. Although hard evidence is lacking, it is possible that a visiting artist could have worked with Moore to develop his ideas. Among the artists who came to the picturesque Southwest every summer, a likely candidate would have been E. A. Burbank who painted for Lorenzo Hubbell many of the pictures of rugs which are still on the walls of Ganado.

Moore's story ends abruptly. As a result of a financial scandal, he and his wife left the Reservation suddenly. Jess Molohon, their store manager, took over Crystal, and nothing further is known of them. The patterns that Moore had developed continued to be woven into the mid-1940s and survived as important influences in other areas of the Reservation. As we have shown, his catalogs remain unique documentary sources of Indian rug design.

Figure 3. Plate from C. N. Cotton's 1896 catalog of Navajo weaving. Hubbell Trading Post National Historic Site. Kent Bush, photographer.

Figure 4. Plate from C. N. Cotton's 1896 catalog of Navajo
weaving. Hubbell Trading Post National Historic Site. Kent Bush,
photographer.

Figure 5.   Plate from C. N. Cotton's 1896 catalog of Navajo weaving. Hubbell Trading Post National Historic Site. Kent Bush, photographer.

Figure 6.   Plate from C. N. Cotton's 1896 catalog of Navajo
weaving. Hubbell Trading Post National Historic Site. Kent Bush,
photographer.

Figure 7. Plate from C. N. Cotton's 1896 catalog of Navajo weaving. Hubbell Trading Post National Historic Site. Kent Bush, photographer.

Figure 8. Plate from John B. Moore's catalog on Navajo weaving, 1911. Original catalogs in collection of Maxwell Museum, University of New Mexico. Michael Mouchette, photographer.

Figure 9. Plate from John B. Moore's catalog on Navajo weaving, 1903. Original catalogs in collection of Maxwell Museum, University of New Mexico. Michael Mouchette, photographer.

Figure 10. Plate from John B. Moore's catalog on Navajo weaving, 1903. Original catalogs in collection of Maxwell Museum, University of New Mexico. Michael Mouchette, photographer.

Figure 11. Plate from John B. Moore's catalog on Navajo weaving, 1903. Original catalogs in collection of Maxwell Museum, University of New Mexico. Michael Mouchette, photographer.

Figure 12. Plate from John B. Moore's catalog on Navajo weaving, 1903. Original catalogs in collection of Maxwell Museum, University of New Mexico. Michael Mouchette, photographer.

Figure 13. Plate from John B. Moore's catalog on Navajo weaving, 1903. Original catalogs in collection of Maxwell Museum, University of New Mexico. Michael Mouchette, photographer.

Figure 14. Plate from John B. Moore's catalog on Navajo weaving, 1911. Original catalogs in collection of Maxwell Museum, University of New Mexico. Michael Mouchette, photographer.

Figure 15. Plate from John B. Moore's catalog on Navajo
weaving, 1911. Original catalogs in collection of Maxwell
Museum, University of New Mexico. Michael Mouchette, photographer.

Figure 16. Plate from John B. Moore's catalog on Navajo weaving, 1911. Original catalogs in collection of Maxwell Museum, University of New Mexico. Michael Mouchette, photographer.

Figure 17. Plate from John B. Moore's catalog on Navajo
weaving, 1911. Original catalogs in collection of Maxwell
Museum, University of New Mexico. Michael Mouchette, photographer.

Figure 18. Plate from John B. Moore's catalog on Navajo weaving, 1911. Original catalogs in collection of Maxwell Museum, University of New Mexico. Michael Mouchette, photographer.

Figure 19. Plate from John B. Moore's catalog on Navajo weaving, 1911. Original catalogs in collection of Maxwell Museum, University of New Mexico. Michael Mouchette, photographer.

Figure 20. Plate from John B. Moore's catalog on Navajo
weaving, 1911. Original catalogs in collection of Maxwell
Museum, University of New Mexico. Michael Mouchette, photographer.

Figure 21. Plate from John B. Moore's catalog on Navajo
weaving, 1911. Original catalogs in collection of Maxwell
Museum, University of New Mexico. Michael Mouchette, photographer.

Figure 22. Plate from John B. Moore's catalog on Navajo weaving, 1911. Original catalogs in collection of Maxwell Museum, University of New Mexico. Michael Mouchette, photographer.

Figure 23. Plate from John B. Moore's catalog on Navajo weaving, 1911. Original catalogs in collection of Maxwell Museum, University of New Mexico. Michael Mouchette, photographer.

Figure 24. Plate from John B. Moore's catalog on Navajo weaving, 1911. Original catalogs in collection of Maxwell Museum, University of New Mexico. Michael Mouchette, photographer.

Figure 25. Plate from John B. Moore's catalog on Navajo weaving, 1911. Original catalogs in collection of Maxwell Museum, University of New Mexico. Michael Mouchette, photographer.

Figure 26. Plate from John B. Moore's catalog on Navajo weaving, 1911. Original catalogs in collection of Maxwell Museum, University of New Mexico. Michael Mouchette, photographer.

Figure 27. Plate from John B. Moore's catalog on Navajo weaving, 1911. Original catalogs in collection of Maxwell Museum, University of New Mexico. Michael Mouchette, photographer.

Figure 28. Plate from John B. Moore's catalog on Navajo weaving, 1903. Original catalogs in collection of Maxwell Museum, University of New Mexico. Michael Mouchette, photographer.

Figure 29. Plate from John B. Moore's catalog on Navajo weaving, 1911. Original catalogs in collection of Maxwell Museum, University of New Mexico. Michael Mouchette, photographer.

Figure 30. Plate from John B. Moore's catalog on Navajo weaving, 1911. Original catalogs in collection of Maxwell Museum, University of New Mexico. Michael Mouchette, photographer.

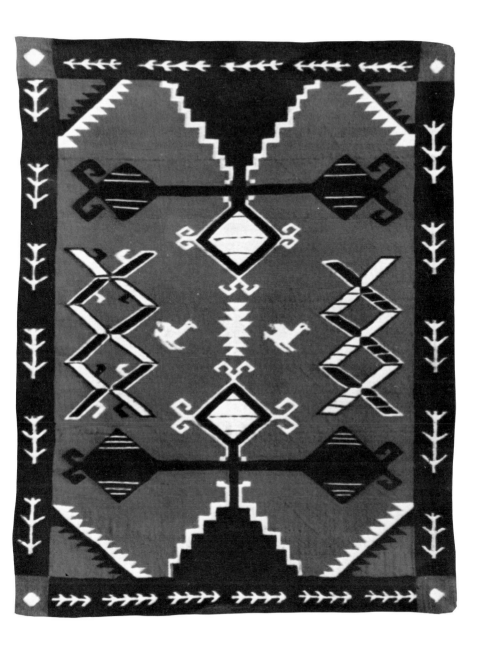

Figure 31. Plate from John B. Moore's catalog on Navajo weaving, 1911. Original catalogs in collection of Maxwell Museum, University of New Mexico. Michael Mouchette, photographer.

Figure 32.   Navajo wedding baskets, c. 1900 to 1930. Maxwell
Museum, University of New Mexico. Jim Bechdel, photographer.

Figure 33. Oriental rug, Bergamo, Turkey, late nineteenth century. Pioneers Museum, Colorado Springs.

Figure 34.   E. S. Frost and Co., Turkish hook rug stencils, 1863 to 1900. Henry Ford Greenfield Village Museum. Jim Bechdel, photographer.

5

George Bloomfield
and Two Grey Hills

When George Bloomfield bought the trading post at Toadlena, New Mexico, in 1911, like J. B. Moore at Crystal on the other side of the Chuska Mountains, he found the weaving quality very poor. In an effort to improve the textiles in his area, he spent a great deal of time examining the rugs brought to his post, and took a personal interest in explaining to each weaver the defects he had spotted and how they might be corrected. With Ed Davies of the neighboring trading post of Two Grey Hills, Bloomfield was instrumental in improving local rugs.

Novices are often under the mistaken impression that the term Two Grey Hills refers to the color and pattern of the rugs bearing that name. In fact, the "two grey hills" are actual landmarks near the trading post, but are not depicted in any of the rugs from this area.

The Two Grey Hills style is well known for simple, harmonious color combinations—well carded grays and beiges and rich medium browns as well as black and white. Plate 9 shows the typical coloration. [When Bloomfield arrived, the story goes, the weavers in the area supposedly had a natural dislike for red (McNitt:260).] The warm beige is a natural wool. This variety of sheep was evidently common all over the Reservation between 1920 and 1940, for we see it in the weaving from other locations as well.

However, only at Two Grey Hills was this camel color deliberately fostered, so that today it appears there exclusively.

Don Smouse, the trader at Borrego Pass, New Mexico, who married Bloomfield's daughter, assured me that no dyes were used on the wool at Toadlena. The staff at the trading post spent many hours sorting through bags of wool collecting just the right colors for distribution to the best weavers. Smouse even brought a small flock of the distinctive camel-colored sheep with him when he took over the trading post at Borrego Pass, but predators destroyed them before he could get a Two Grey Hills style established there (Personal communication: 1975).

The essence of Two Grey Hills is elaboration and tight organization. Usually the four corners of the main field are emphasized (Figures 35 to 39). These rugs are characterized by wide or multiple borders, the same on all four sides, each with a different motif. Usually we see an outer black stripe followed by a broad inner band of white with a simple running figure often outlined in another color projecting into this white area (Figure 36). Frequently, this border design is a scroll or fret (Figures 37 and 38). About 90 percent of the time the central area is a medium tone, a carded gray, beige, or brown (Figure 38). There is either a central diamond, as in Figure 36, or the rug may be divided in half (Figures 38 and 39).

Because of the stylistic similarity, a connection seems probable between early Crystal rugs and Two Grey Hills. The link is clearly shown in Figure 35, a rug purchased before 1933 by Mrs. Dwight B. Heard and now in the Heard Museum, Phoenix. Here we see a border that is an exact interpretation of the tuning fork pattern with an elaborate center found in J. B. Moore's catalog (Figure 29). This rug is also especially interesting because of its quite unusual predominantly black ground. Two Grey Hills rug designs are also very reminiscent of Crystal's oriental rug look, filled with hooks and many small floating motifs in addition to large central medallions.

Figure 35. Two Grey Hills rug with J. B. Moore border, collected before 1933 by Mrs. Dwight Heard. Heard Museum, Phoenix. Jerry Jacka, photographer.

Figure 36.   Two Grey Hills rug, c. 1920 to 1940. Heard Museum, Phoenix. Jerry Jacka, photographer.

Figure 37.   Two Grey Hills rug, c. 1920 to 1940. Heard Museum, Phoenix. Jerry Jacka, photographer.

Figure 38.   Two Grey Hills rug, c. 1920 to 1940. Heard Museum, Phoenix. Jerry Jacka, photographer.

Figure 39. Two Grey Hills rug, c. 1920 to 1940. Heard Museum,
Phoenix, Jerry Jacka, photographer.

The rug in the color illustration is also interesting for its unique pattern. It was purchased at the Newcomb trading post in 1929, the same post where Hosteen Klah and his family developed ceremonial pattern weaving (see Chapter 9). So it is not surprising to see four *yei* (supernatural figures) springing from four points of the central eight-pointed star. Again, the four corners are emphasized.

By 1925 the traditional Two Grey Hills style was well developed. It has remained very much the same in appearance to this day, having changed less than the weaving of any other sector of the Reservation. The weavers have conserved a style that has been very popular and has provided ample financial reward. Weavers such as Bessie Many Goats and Daisy Togulchee have greatly influenced the increasingly fine weave of today's rugs. Indeed, Two Grey Hills rugs have become vehicles for the weavers' virtuosity.

A collector should bear in mind that the primary difference between a Two Grey Hills woven today and one manufactured in 1930 is the quality of wool (see Chapter 3) and the fine weave of modern rugs that greatly surpasses older examples. We see finer and finer spinning and weaving techniques producing display pieces of well over one hundred wefts per inch.

It would also be useful to remember that large amounts of gray and black alone do not make a Two Grey Hills, since these colors, with red and white, were commonly found all over the Reservation from 1900 to 1940. A true Two Grey Hills will manifest some stylistic elements that we have discussed here and others that may be found among our illustrations.

6

Lorenzo Hubbell of Ganado and His Trading Empire

Lorenzo Hubbell opened his trading post at Ganado, Arizona, in 1876 or 1878; the exact date is uncertain. The post had been known as Pueblo Colorado, but Hubbell renamed it for his friend Ganado Mucho, "Many Herds," a local chief. Able, talented, and enthusiastic, Hubbell soon prospered and opened other posts at Chinle, Black Mountain, Cornfields, Nazlini, Keams Canyon, Oraibi, Cedar Springs, and Piñon Springs. (He was extremely hospitable and entertained many famous tourists, including President Theodore Roosevelt and his family. For a full account of Hubbell's life see Frank McNitt's *The Indian Traders.*)

Hubbell was interested—as were J. B. Moore and other traders on the Reservation—in adapting Navajo weaving to the tastes of the Anglo buying public. He preferred the old Classic blanket patterns in black, red, blue, and white. These were generally fine, blanketlike textiles, frequently with a narrow striped background with a large stepped diamond (Plate 10). They are often called *Moki* or *Hopi style* because they resemble Hopi blankets commonly composed of dark brown and indigo blue stripes. The majority of Hubbell "revival" pieces are in Germantown yarn.

One method that Hubbell used to stimulate weaving in the style he preferred was having artists such as E. A.

Burbank paint small simplified blanket patterns. These illustrations were then hung on the trading post walls to encourage the local weavers to reproduce them. During his travels across the United States, Burbank looked for good examples of blankets in private collections to paint for Hubbell; but after one disappointing trip, he suggested that Hubbell send him photographs of the blankets being woven at the post so that he could render them in oils. Plates 11a through d show four paintings from Ganado that exhibit these Hubbell Revival patterns.

Although the blue and black striped background blankets are more familiar to collectors, we find among the revived styles the Classic women's dresses (Plate 11c), the chief's pattern blanket, and wearing blankets (Plate 11d). These are duplications of early nineteenth-century pattern and design, *not materials*. These revival pieces are almost always woven with analine-dyed Germantown yarns, not raveled material or real indigo-dyed handspun. In this context it is interesting to note that the surviving examples of Hubbell Revival blankets are in pristine condition, almost as if the purchasers had acquired them as collectors items in the realization that true Classic period weaving was already rare and expensive.

Unfortunately, the revival style was not popular. Herman Schweizer, the arts and crafts buyer for the Fred Harvey Company, wrote to Hubbell in 1905 that the "shawl" patterns wouldn't sell at any price. Nevertheless, as late as 1909, Hubbell was writing to a lady customer still extolling the beauty of his blanket revivals. Even today customers may purchase blankets woven from the paintings hanging in the old trading post, now a National Park Service Monument. But now an important difference is that modern weavers use all hundspun yarns.

A series of postcards dating between 1903 and 1911 and showing weavers from Ganado at the old Alvarado Hotel in Albuquerque, indicates that the famous rug styles had already been established. By the first decade of the twentieth century, Ganado weavers were producing patterns that would be popular for the next twenty years.

Chapter 6

Roughly half the paintings at the post are in the new rug style with large bold patterns floating against plain white, gray, or red grounds (Plate 12). The design in 12a is remarkably similar to one of the rugs in C. N. Cotton's catalogs (Figure 3). This pattern, as well as that in Plate 12b of two stepped diamonds, remains popular throughout the entire period. Many of the patterns show a similarity to those adopted by J. B. Moore. The border in Figure 14, the wavy line, becomes especially prevalent at Ganado, as does the double diamond as a central pattern (Figure 16). Even the storm pattern becomes popular. I surmise that Moore's success with his designs prompted Hubbell to direct his weavers to the new oriental patterns that were becoming popular with buyers, probably with the behind-the-scenes encouragement of wholesalers such as Cotton. However, my examination of the Hubbell correspondence at the University of Arizona, Tucson, has not provided evidence that Moore and Hubbell acted together to spread the style.

The correspondence between Hubbell and various dealers in other parts of the country, during the important formative years from 1900 to 1910, is, nevertheless, quite interesting. The rug business was booming, and Hubbell was quite pleased with his success. He continually encouraged dealers all over the country to handle Navajo weaving, although, he says, for some reason he had never been able to interest businessmen in the South.

In 1908, an otherwise slow, slightly depressed year for the national economy, Hubbell grossed $45,000 in the rug business, with only $3,000 worth of rugs returned. The fact that Hubbell allowed dealers to return unsold weaving at the end of the year indicates that style was very closely tied to the public's buying patterns. Rugs were generally returned because their color was *unpopular*. So Hubbell would instruct his employees accordingly: they were to purchase from the weavers only those colors the dealers preferred. At that time, the two principal ground colors were gray and white with figures in black and red. (White rugs with gray and black figures were considered appropriate for the bathroom.)

Navajo weaving design was becoming definitely tied to the interior decorating tastes of Chicago and Los Angeles. These market fluctuations were undoubtedly very hard on the weavers, who might bring in a good rug only to find that the trader was buying rugs exclusively in a different color that year.

In 1909, we find blankets with brown backgrounds mentioned for the first time, as gray goes out of favor. Hubbell orders larger quantities of cardinal red dye, for red becomes the preferred ground. At about this time, he is making a greater profit on saddle blankets than on rugs. Averaging from 30 to 36 inches wide by 50 to 60 inches long, they are still being used on horses, not as throw rugs, and are his best sellers at seventy-five cents to a dollar a pound. This same year, Hubbell reports that a few weavers are still making bayeta blankets, two or three a year, and he has one for sale at $75 that measures four-and-a-half by seven-and-a-half feet.

As we have already noted, paintings and documents are indispensable research sources for periods like the Transitional. But for an analysis of the rug patterns popular from 1920 to 1940 at Ganado, we are fortunate to have the actual Hubbell Trading Post weaving collection to examine. These textiles were in continuous use at the Hubbell home, and provide a well dated if somewhat stained and worn sample. The National Park Service has had copies made of most of the floor rugs, so that the originals may be preserved in storage. But all over the house, we may find rugs, bedspreads, chairbacks, and portieres (Figure 40).

Many aspects of Ganado style were formed in the Transitional period. But the large bold patterns tended to become smaller and more elaborate during the 1920s and 1930s. Border designs, like many at Crystal, were based on basket patterns, especially the stepped triangle. At Ganado we see a right-angled type (Figure 47). The most common border is a solid stripe of black or black and red, either on all four sides or only at the top and bottom (Figure 44). We may also see a tab or ribbonlike border, another influence of basketry design (Figure 45). One of the most distinctive

Figure 40. Bedroom at Hubbell Trading Post, Ganado, Arizona, with reproduction rug on floor, and an old Chinle on the brass bed. María Jorrín Bauer, photographer.

features of the borders of Ganado rugs during this period is the difference between the sides and the top and bottom (Figure 47). They may be totally different in design or proportion. A latter example is the zigzag borders in Figure 51.

If we examine the fields of Ganado rugs, we find a duplication of nineteenth-century blanket motifs in overall diamonds (Figures 41 and 42), the large X shape either relatively simple as in Figure 43, or with every color outlined as in Figure 44. But by far the most important design layouts of this period are double and triple central diamonds or crosses as illustrated in Figures 45 to 50. (Both types relate to turn-of-the-century paintings at the trading post, Plates 12a, b, and d.) Often when there are three central figures, the middle one is smaller than the other two, as in Figure 50, and, especially, in the rug on the bedroom floor in Figure 40. Many of the diamonds are embellished with numerous small hooks as in Moore's Crystal patterns (Figure 49). The popular cross motif we see at Ganado is the Greek cross, as we have mentioned earlier, a design derived from Navajo basketry and the symbol of Spider Woman, a Navajo diety. Often this cross has squares at the end of each arm.

A distinctive Ganado motif, not found at the other posts, is the design composed of little stepped hourglasses (Figure 51). This is also found in one of the paintings, Plate 12c. Sometimes the entire design is built of combinations of hourglasses in various colors and sometimes it is found alone as a background filler.

Plate 13 illustrates the customary Ganado spectrum, black, white, red, gray, and the camel beige we have explained earlier as chiefly found now at Two Grey Hills, after having been prevalent in rugs all over the Reservation in the first half of the twentieth century. But it is the dark red that has become characteristic of Ganado, large areas of it common to rugs of the Transitional and Modern periods. During the intermediate period we have been discussing, a more balanced color combination was popular, and we find examples of many rugs woven exclusively in black, white, and gray. Ganado red, famous for its richness, is supposed to have been passed through two dye baths. Earlier reds are not as deep and maroon, and many have subsequently faded to a lovely strawberry hue.

Pre-1940 Ganado rugs can be recognized by their overall verticality—two or three medallions running down the center, large X shapes, and zigzags from top to bottom on each side. Modern or post-1940 Ganados, on the other hand, usually have large central medallions and strong motifs in each of the four corners. In fact, they are rather like Two Grey Hills rugs with the addition of deep red instead of brown. This change, quite apparent when modern rugs are compared with the examples on these pages, probably resulted from the increasing popularity and prestige of Two Grey Hills that influenced Ganado weavers to modify their own style.

Much of the widespread popularity of Ganado rugs between 1900 and 1940 can be attributed to Herman Schweizer, the buyer for the Fred Harvey Company, who had contracted with Hubbell to supply most of the rugs sold at the Harvey stores. Both men had an eye for quality and paid well for good rugs and blankets. Hubbell himself was an astute promoter who was well known for producing large custom-ordered rugs as well as pieces of consistently high quality. The fact that he owned so many trading posts is probably also responsible for the quantity of Ganados. Many of these posts were run by Hubbell's relatives and friends, and his taste prevailed among them all. A letter from Lorenzo, Jr., who was at the Keams Canyon post in 1908, suggests how widely the popular and dynamic Ganado style had spread through the Hubbell posts. In an effort to recover a rug mistakenly sent to the main post, Lorenzo, Jr., sent a sketch to help identify it. In that drawing we see a Keams Canyon rug clearly in the Ganado style.

To summarize, the primary change we should be aware of in identifying Ganados before and after World War II is the shift in patterns from large floating and blocky oriental designs to more refined vertical motifs, and finally to centrally organized Two Grey Hills layouts. In addition to noting the changes in wool type that we discussed earlier, we should look out for a preponderance of red early in the century, less red in the 1920s and 1930s, and finally a return to more red that deepens to maroon after 1940.

Figure 41.   Ganado rug, c. 1920 to 1940. Hubbell Trading Post National Historic Site. María Jorrín Bauer, photographer.

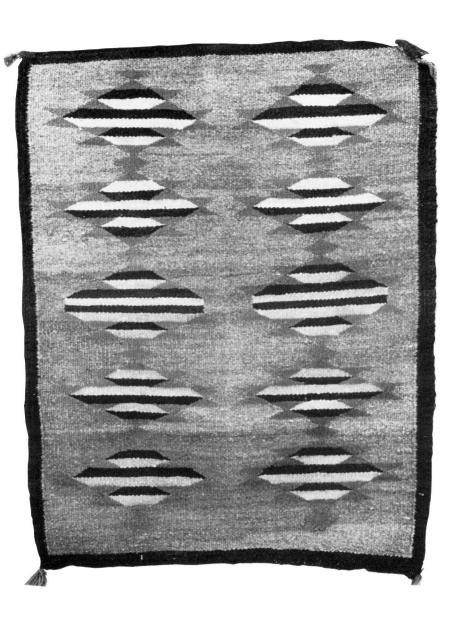

Figure 42.   Ganado rug, c. 1920 to 1940. Hubbell Trading Post
National Historic Site. María Jorrín Bauer, photographer.

Figure 43.   Ganado rug, c. 1920 to 1940. Hubbell Trading Post
National Historic Site. María Jorrín Bauer, photographer.

Figure 44. Ganado rug, c. 1920 to 1940. Hubbell Trading Post
National Historic Site. María Jorrín Bauer, photographer.

Figure 45.   Ganado rug, c. 1920 to 1940. Hubbell Trading Post
National Historic Site. María Jorrín Bauer, photographer.

Figure 46.   Ganado rug, c. 1920 to 1940. Hubbell Trading Post
National Historic Site. María Jorrín Bauer, photographer.

Figure 47. Ganado rug, c. 1920 to 1940. Hubbell Trading Post National Historic Site. María Jorrín Bauer, photographer.

Figure 48.   Ganado rug, c. 1920 to 1940. Hubbell Trading Post
National Historic Site. María Jorrín Bauer, photographer.

Figure 49.   Ganado rug, c. 1920 to 1940. Hubbell Trading Post National Historic Site. María Jorrín Bauer, photographer.

Figure 50. Ganado rug, c. 1920 to 1940. Hubbell Trading Post
National Historic Site. María Jorrín Bauer, photographer.

Figure 51.   Ganado rug, c. 1920 to 1940. Hubbell Trading Post
National Historic Site. María Jorrín Bauer, photographer.

7

Wheelwright, McSparron, and the Chinle Revival

Still another area of the Reservation where a trader successfully attempted to alter the course of Navajo weaving was Chinle, Arizona, situated at the mouth of Canyon de Chelly, spectacular for its scenery and Anasazi ruins. Lorenzo Hubbell had owned the trading post there until 1917, his weavers producing rugs in the Ganado style. With the opening of roads in the 1920s that made the Navajo country more accessible than ever before, tourists began to visit the area more and to stay at the Thunderbird Inn at Chinle.

At about this time, a prominent visitor to the Southwest, Mary Cabot Wheelwright, an enthusiastic patron of Native American art, who ran an Indian crafts shop in Boston and was later to found the Museum of Navajo Ceremonial Art in Santa Fe, began working with Cozy McSparron, the trader who followed Hubbell, to improve weaving quality at the Chinle post.

Miss Wheelwright objected to harsh aniline colors and oriental rug designs in Native-American weaving, and sought a return to nineteenth-century Classic blanket styles and an improvement in the craft processes themselves. She would send color photographs and oil paintings of fine examples of Classic period weaving (generally with horizontal banded patterns) to McSparron for distribution to his best weavers. McNitt reports that McSparron and another trader at Chinle, Camille García, actually bought thirty-eight old Navajo rugs and Mexican blankets to show the weavers (McNitt 1962:251). To encourage the project, Miss Wheelwright even supplied the funds to purchase the weavers' initial efforts, so that no matter how unsuccessful they were the trader could buy them, and thereby induce more weavers to try the new style. Eventually the number of weavers who took up the revival patterns increased with the financial incentive to do so. At times, however, their willingness to please led to unforseen problems: they would follow the photographs so closely that sometimes they duplicated mistakes in the pictures, such as corners that had been folded down.

At first, many of the revival rugs were woven with aniline dyes, generally with a lot of red, sometimes with several different bright colors. However, after five or ten years these brightly dyed and banded rugs disappeared. For in addition to reviving traditional patterns, Miss Wheelwright encouraged the improvement of Chinle dyes. Some older weavers in the area remembered the recipes for extracting dyes from local plants—perhaps because of their continued use in basketry and leather dyeing—and in time more and more native dyes were used with the old patterns. Many women joined enthusiastically in the dye project, and began finding new plants and inventing recipes that had never been tried before.

And so Chinle's distinctive palette evolved: white, black, the yellows and browns of southwestern desert plants, and lovely delicate shades of green, lavender, pink, and un-carded gray (Plate 14). At first, the dealers and wholesalers at Gallup objected to the new style, but their resistance was gradually overcome. The borderless revival rugs grew in popularity with Anglo buyers, probably not only because the golds and browns were reminders of the desert landscape they had recently traveled through, but also because the subtle earth tones suited modern furniture extremely well.

With the continued financial support of Miss Wheel-

wright, Chinle remained a center for weaving experimenta-
tion. The weavers were to receive some of the first
experimental wool and sheep from the Fort Wingate
Laboratory. Moreover, Miss Wheelwright even asked the
DuPont Company to develop some muted, natural-looking
colors, in an effort to achieve the softness of vegetal dyes in
especially difficult to attain reds and blues. The results were
dyes that used chrome as a mordant (Plate 14). Most of the
chrome dyeing was done by Inja McSparron, the Chinle
trader's wife (Stoller 1976:458). But chrome dyes presented
problems: they require acetic acid, which, though fairly
mild, can still cause burns. In addition, the wool that has
been treated with chrome dye will yellow if it is exposed to
sunlight during the dyeing process. For these reasons
chrome dyes did not catch on with Navajo weavers, and, as
as result, only seventy-five rugs were manufactured (Maxwell: personal communication 1975).

In Figures 52 to 54 we see some of the most common
designs of Chinle's early formative period. One of the most
distinctive is an asymmetrical barbed stripe, resembling the
Amtrak logo, frequently found in weaving of the 1880s
(Figure 52). It is interesting to see that it was the more
simple blanket patterns that were duplicated, not the
rather elaborate, intricate styles also common to Classic
weaving. And although the Chinle weavers used
nineteenth-century banded designs, their pastel wools gave
the old Navajo patterns quite a different look from the bold
Classic red, white, and blue we have seen in Plate 1.

Nevertheless, the Chinle style spread to other posts. Bill
and Sallie Lippincott, a young couple who had served as
rangers at Canyon de Chelly, bought the trading post at
Wide Ruins in 1938. they had seen the revival style first-
hand at Chinle and decided to do something similar. At
first they purchased only plain striped rugs, later rugs dyed
with the same vegetal dyes at Chinle. Gradually they
encouraged their weavers to try new dye recipes of their
own and to begin adding design elements to the striped
patterns. Rugs were brought in from Chinle and displayed
at the Wide Ruins store for the weavers to admire. Finally,

Figure 52.   Chinle Revival rug, c. 1930 to 1940. Hubbell Trading
Post National Historic Site. María Jorrín Bauer, photographer.

Figure 53. Chinle Revival rug, c. 1930 to 1940. Hubbell Trading Post National Historic Site. María Jorrín Bauer, photographer.

Figure 54.   Chinle Revival rug, c. 1930 to 1940. Hubbell Trading
Post National Historic Site. María Jorrín Bauer, photographer.

the weaving instructor from Fort Wingate was brought in to teach a course, the Lippincotts agreeing to buy all the rugs that were produced (Stoller 1976:558–59). Through these slow methods the Chinle Revival style was firmly established at Wide Ruins. In the 1940s it spread to Crystal, replacing J. B. Moore's patterns that had been woven continuously until that time. Today, of course, the Chinle Revival style is found all over the Reservation.

8

Tees Nos Pos, Red Lake, and Tuba City

Gilbert Maxwell, trading in the Southwest after World War II, said that 75 percent of the rugs woven then could not be identified as originating from a particular trading post (Maxwell 1963: 52). This was probably true between 1900 and 1940, also. The trading posts we have been discussing, where traders were actively at work to change weaving technique and design, became regional centers from which ideas rippled through the surrounding country. Only those rugs containing ample, clearly identifiable features can be attributed to one region. But, as we have seen, weavers in many parts of the Reservation incorporated from various sources individual motifs that seemed to be popular with buyers elsewhere.

Today we find that the idea of regional styles, which was always a shaky concept, has completely changed. There is much greater communication on the Navajo Reservation than ever before, and most of the publications on weaving are bought by the weavers and serve as their models. Also, fewer women are learning the craft as children at their mothers' side. They learn later in life at a special weaving class at a tribal chapter house or in a community college, frequently working in styles drawn from all over the Reservation.

Nevertheless, there are a few areas that we should

include in our discussion even though their rugs are stylistically less significant than those from the aforementioned major trading posts. The most important of these is Tees Nos Pos in the Four Corners area, where the borders of New Mexico, Arizona, Utah, and Colorado meet. Here, an early missionary—recalled only as Mrs. Wilson—is credited with developing the local style sometime before 1905 (McNitt 1962: 343). However, from descriptions of the style and from the photographs of H. B. Noel, the trader's display at the Shiprock Fairs from 1909 to 1915 (Figure 55), we can tell that Tees Nos Pos rugs of the Transitional Period were woven in a distinctively zigzag outline style, apparently derived from earlier Eyedazzlers (Plate 2). Although every element was outlined with a different color, the Tees rugs were much more subtly colored than the Eyedazzlers. The Tees Nos Pos style that collectors know today is somewhat related to the earlier outline style, but now contains many small complex filler elements. The

Figure 55.   H. B. Noel's booth at the Shiprock Fair, 1911 or 1912. Postcard in the collection of the Maxwell Museum, University of New Mexico.

design explodes all over the field (Figure 56). Although post-1940 Tees Nos Pos rugs look as if they may have derived from a plate in C. N. Cotton's 1896 catalog (Figure 7), I could find no documented examples prior to World War II to prove the connection. Modern Tees rugs are woven primarily with commercial yarns, while old Tees were made of aniline-dyed handspun.

In 1886, the brothers David and William Babbitt arrived in Flagstaff, where they became ranchers and merchants. They got into the Indian trading business almost by accident, when the trader who operated the post at Red Lake was shot and killed. Because he had owed them so much money, the Babbitts took over the post to insure their investment, and it turned out to be the first in a series of trading posts managed by the family in the late nineteenth and early twentieth centuries.

The business records kept by the Babbitts reveal only how many rugs were sold, not what they looked like. For examples of rug design at Red Lake, we are indebted to an early tourist to the Southwest, Earle R. Forrest, who took a number of photographs of rugs he had purchased at the trading post. The Red Lake rug bought there in 1908 clearly demonstrates that the Transitional style, with large coarse figures against a solid ground, had become popular all over the Reservation (Figure 57).

Two popular rug designs have become associated with Tuba City, the storm pattern and vertically running diamonds. The former design had appeared in J. B. Moore's catalog in 1911 (see Figure 15) and was apparently woven in the Crystal area as well. Kate Peck Kent says that the storm pattern was used as a stationery design by the Babbitts in the 1890s. The running diamonds motif is composed of connecting open center squares, often in two colors as in Figure 58, a rug woven in 1914 for the retirement of a Phelps Dodge employee. Only a detail of the 99- by 145-inch rug is shown here. These open squares appear on many Babbitt trading post rugs, from as early as 1908 to the 1930s, as we see in Figure 59, a rug collected in 1932.

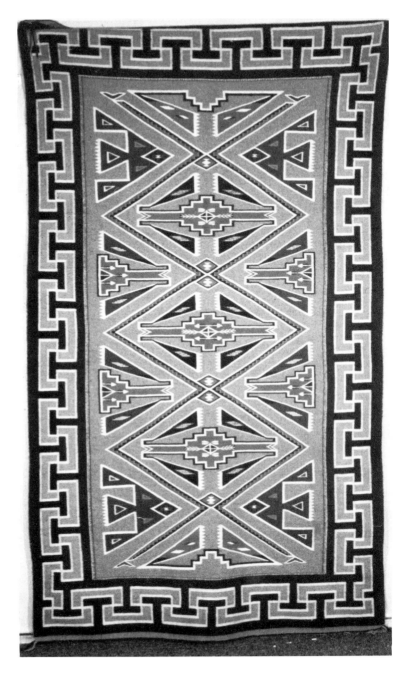

Figure 56. Tees Nos Pos rug, c. 1950. Maxwell Museum, University of New Mexico.

Figure 57. Rug purchased in 1908 at Red Lake Trading Post, Arizona, by Earl R. Forrest. Museum of Northern Arizona, Flagstaff.

Figure 58.   Detail rug woven in 1914 near Tuba City, Arizona.
Museum of Northern Arizona, Flagstaff.

Figure 59.   Rug bought in 1932 at Richardson Brothers Post at
Tuba City. Heard Museum, Phoenix. Jerry Jacka, photographer.

9

Pictorial and Ceremonial Rugs

In our discussion so far, we have concentrated predominantly on geometric, nonrepresentational designs in Navajo weaving. However, pictorial elements, identifiable depictions of animals or people, are found occasionally in the earliest examples of datable, intact pieces. For example, the blanket taken from the body of White Antelope, a Cheyenne chief killed in the Massacre at Sand Creek, Colorado (1864), contains a pattern of small seated ducks, so small they are hardly noticeable in the overall design.

An interesting group of rugs, identified as having been made in the Mancos, Colorado, area around 1900, contains black human and animal figures woven on a white ground, all in the coarse, kempy wool of the period (Figure 60). During the Germantown and Transitional periods, birds, bows, arrows, and weaving equipment, especially combs used to beat down the wefts, are frequently used as fillers. However, after the 1920s it is unusual to find geometric and pictorial styles combined.

Patriotic themes are also part of the history of Navajo weaving, perhaps developed for army officers stationed in the Southwest. A photograph dated 1873 shows Governor Arny seated next to a Navajo weaver with a flag rug on her loom. This, the first documented, wholly pictorial piece of

Figure 60. Cow pictorial rug, made in Mancos, Colorado, c. 1900 to 1910. Taylor Museum, Colorado Springs Fine Arts Center.

Navajo weaving, marks the beginning of a long tradition of patriotic designs. Flags are still woven today, as are American eagles, some designs taken directly from U.S. coins.

In addition, almost every trader in Navajo country had a rug woven for the wall of his store with the name of his trading post or his personal initials. Likewise, many ranchers had their names or cattle brands woven to order. But pictorial weaving often goes its own individualistic way with motifs chosen at the weavers' pleasure. Not only did they depict the plants and animals they saw around them, but often they would copy labels on cans and packaged goods on the trading post shelves; the letters were pleasant abstract patterns with great aesthetic appeal. (As true of other rugs from 1920 to 1940, the best way of dating these textiles is by wool type.)

During the 1920s and 1930s in the Flagstaff area, a distinctive style developed around the use of Hopi designs. In some instances complete Hopi kachinas were depicted, in others prehistoric pottery motifs. Figure 61 is a classic Awatovi pottery pattern skillfully adapted from a bowl to a two-dimensional rug.

This brings us to the question of religious subject matter in Navajo weaving. Since the late nineteenth century, the Navajo have woven rugs for sale to Anglo buyers that incorporate images from Navajo religion. Contrary to the belief of some, these textiles do not serve in actual Navajo ceremonies and are not used by the Navajo as prayer rugs. Among the earliest motifs were figures of Navajo supernaturals called *yeis*. Individual yeis were followed by lines of human dancers performing the *Yeibichai* dance from the Night Chant. Many Navajo considered these woven representations to be sacriligious, but the rugs sold, and, as a result, so-called ceremonial weaving has continued to be produced ever since (Amsden 1934:106).

Sandpaintings, or dry paintings, to be more accurate, are an integral part of Navajo *sings* or curing rituals. Executed in colored sands and vegetal materials, they are meant to be transitory, to be used and destroyed in the space of a

Figure 61. Navajo rug with prehistoric Hopi pottery design (Awatovi type) made for Chee Dodge, c. 1924. Museum of Northern Arizona, Flagstaff.

day. However, a number of Navajo medicine men have cooperated with researchers to record the rituals and the dry paintings associated with them. The first dry painting rug was made in 1896 near Chaco Canyon (Wheat 1975). Continued cooperation has led to the publication of chantways and reproductions of dry paintings in books. Today rugs that reproduce these religious images are often based on published illustrations; but others are still based on the weaver's memory of ceremonies she has witnessed.

Many years ago, Hosteen Klah, an important medicine man near the trading post of Newcomb, New Mexico, began to weave ceremonial tapestries at the suggestion of Franc Newcomb, the trader's wife. Klah wove his first rug, "The Whirling Logs," in 1920. His personal style was distinctive from the beginning. He used only backgrounds of tan undyed wool from the bellies of brown sheep. His dyes were carefully prepared from local plants and indigo and cochineal, although later he would come to use commercial dyes. He wove exceptionally large rugs, about twelve feet by twelve or thirteen, on specially constructed looms.

Klah's family also took part. Under his direction, his mother and his nieces, Mrs. Sam and Mrs. Jim, also began weaving ceremonial rugs. He was known to bless them and their work constantly, for they were producing weavings in spite of the belief by many medicine men that misfortune would befall the weavers and the tribe for making exact reproductions of sandpaintings. Evidently Klah's great spiritual powers were enough to prevent any trouble. Plate 15 is the last of the twenty-five ceremonial rugs that Klah wove between 1920 and his death in 1936.

Between 1920 and 1940 a rug style developed that is a mixture of pictorial and ceremonial elements (Plate 16). Sacred motifs such as the Corn People are intermingled with birds and sheep. In this way, weavers could satisfy buyers' demands for rugs with religious imagery without the risk of offending the supernaturals.

Since the 1940s there have been many changes in ceremonial rug weaving. Perhaps because he was a medicine man and accustomed to spending a great deal of time preparing for rituals, Klah took so much trouble selecting just the right wool and preparing special dyes. After his death, virtually no weavers of ceremonial rugs used handspun vegetal-dyed wools. From 1940 until today, they have used commercial yarns, although frequently choosing "natural" sand colors for their backgrounds.

Moreover, without the spiritual protection of a medicine man like Hosteen Klah, modern weavers change some details of the sandpainting they copy. It is difficult to say what the weavers of fifty and sixty years ago felt about the work they were doing, but many weavers specializing in ceremonial patterns now do so in spite of great personal discomfort. They think they are performing a sacriligious act, incurring the dislike and resentment of their neighbors. As a result, they may come to believe that they are victims of witchcraft. So, much of the money they earn goes to pay for healing rituals. Therefore, ceremonial rugs tend to be very expensive, reflecting the costs that have been expended not only to induce weavers to undertake the difficult techniques, but also to pay medicine men for the ceremonies to cleanse them.

Afterword

This book has attempted to sort out and trace the origins of regional Navajo rug styles, ironically at a time when the concept of regionalism is dying. But the desire to know exactly where an artistic creation comes from and who the creator was remains a powerful Anglo concern. To the Navajo artist, the act of creation is an end in itself; the final product is less important than the process. This deep difference will always separate the two cultures. There is certainly no evidence that nineteenth-century weaving had specific regional associations. It is only with the turn of the century, under the strong encouragement of a few Anglo traders, that regionally identifiable weaving developed. The very concept of an area designation for rugs is associated with oriental or Near Eastern rug weaving. Perhaps the idea of regionalsim as well as the patterns were oriental in inspiration.

Since Navajo weavers do not work in isolation today, but buy many of the current books and periodicals on their craft, one can say with certainty only that a rug has been woven in the Ganado style or the Two Grey Hills style, not that it was made in that area of the Reservation. And because the Navajo are interested in their past and are constantly reworking old patterns and ideas, perhaps this book will also find its way out on the Reservation and influence some changes in style among weavers.

Bibliography

Amsden, Charles Avery

    1932   "Reviving the Navaho Blanket," *The Masterkey*, Vol. VI, no. 5, 137–49.

    1934   *Navajo Weaving, Its Technic and Its History* (Glorieta, N.M.: Rio Grande Press, Inc.).

Bennett, N. and T. Bighorse

    1971   *Working with the Wool* (Flagstaff: Northland Press).

Blunn, Cecil

    1940   "Navajo Sheep," *Journal of Heredity*, 31:99–112.

Brody, J. J.

    1976   *Between Traditions: Navajo Weaving Toward the End of the Nineteenth Century* (Iowa City: Stamats Publishing Co.).

Cerny, C.

    1975   *Navajo Pictorial Weaving* (Santa Fe: Museum of New Mexico Foundation).

Cotton, C. N.

    1896?   *Indian Traders' Supplies and Navajo Blankets* (Denver: Williamson Haffner Co.)

Dedera, Don

    1975   *Navajo Rugs: How to Find, Evaluate, Buy and Care for Them* (Flagstaff: Northland Press).

Dutton, Bertha

    1961   *Navajo Weaving Today* (Santa Fe: Museum of New Mexico Press).

Grandstaff, James O.

    1941   *Evaluating Fleece Characteristics of Navajo Sheep from a Breeding Standpoint.* Reprint from *Rayon Textile Monthly*, n.p.

    1942   *Wool Characteristics in Relation to Navajo Weaving*

(Washington: U.S. Department of Agriculture Technical Bulletin No. 790).

Hollister, U. S.
1903 *The Navajo and His Blanket* (Denver: United States Colortype Co.)

Hubbell, J. L.
1939 "Fifty Years an Indian Trader," *Touring Topics*, XXII, no. 12:24–35, 51.

James, George W.
1920 *Indian Blankets and Their Makers* (Chicago: A. C. McClurg and Co.).

James, H. L.
1976 *Posts and Rugs: The Story of Navajo Rugs and Their Homes* (Globe: Southwest Parks and Monuments Association).

Kahlenberg, Mary H. and A. Berlant
1972 *The Navajo Blanket* (New York: Praeger Publishers Inc.).
1977 *Walk in Beauty* (Boston: New York Graphic Society).

Kent, Kate P.
1961 *Navajo Weaving* (Phoenix: The Heard Museum).

Maxwell, Gilbert
1963 *Navajo Rugs—Past, Present, and Future* (Palm Desert: Desert-Southwest, Inc.).

McNitt, Frank
1962 *The Indian Traders* (Norman: University of Oklahoma Press).

Mera, H. P.
1948 *Navajo Textile Arts* (Santa Fe: Laboratory of Anthropology).

Moore, J. B.
1903 *Fine Navajo Blankets*
1911 *The Navajo* (Denver: Williamson-Haffner Co.).

Newcomb, F. J.
1964 *Hosteen Klah: Navajo Medicine Man and Sand Painter* (Norman: University of Oklahoma Press).

Pendleton, M.
1974 *Navajo and Hopi Weaving Techniques* (New York: Collier Books).

Reichard, Gladys A.
1963 *Navajo Shepherd and Weaver* (New York: J. J. Augustin).

Rodee, Marian

    1977   *Southwestern Weaving* (Albuquerque: University of New Mexico Press).

Simmons, Katina

    1976   "Oriental Influences in Navajo Rug Design," *Proceedings of the Irene Emery Roundtable,* pp. 445–52.

Stoller, I. P.

    1976   "The Revival Period in Navajo Weaving," *Proceedings of the Irene Emery Roundtable,* pp. 453–66.

Underhill, Ruth

    1953   *Here Come the Navaho* (Lawrence Kansas: Haskell Institute, U.S. Indian Service.)

    1956   *The Navajo* (Norman: University of Oklahoma Press).

Wheat, J. B.

    1975   *Patterns and Sources of Navajo Weaving* (Denver: The Printing Establishment).

    1976   "Documentary Basis for Material Changes and Design Styles in Navajo Blanket Weaving," *Proceedings of the Irene Emery Roundtable,* pp. 425–40.

Index

storm pattern, 23, 67, 93. *See also* pictorial designs
stripes, 2, 3, 11, 58, 65, 66, 68, 85. *See also* geometric designs
swastikas, 23. *See also* geometric designs

Tees Nos Pos Trading Post, 92, 93
terraces, 2. *See also* geometric designs
Toadlena, New Mexico, 57, 58
Togulchee, Daisy, 64
Transhumantes, 12. *See also* sheep
Transitional period, 7–9, 13, 15, 16, 68, 70, 92, 93, 99
triangles, 68. *See also* geometric designs
Tuba City, 23, 93
tuning fork pattern, 21, 58. *See also* geometric designs
Turkey, 22
Two Grey Hills style, 57–64, 70, 71, 105

Underhill, Ruth, 13
United States Department of the Interior, 15

vegetal dyes, 4, 85, 104. *See also* dyes

warps, 16
water bugs, 23. *See also* pictorial designs
wavy lines, 2, 21, 67. *See also* geometric designs
wefts, 16, 99
Western Reservation, 23
Wheat, J. B., 103
Wheelwright, Mary Cabot, 83, 84, 85
Wheelwright Museum, 17
Wide Ruins, 85, 89
Wilkin, Joe, 19
wool, 1, 11, 12. *See also* fiber
World War II, 15, 71, 91, 93

X shapes, 69, 70. *See also* geometric designs
yarns, 4, 5, 104; Germantown, 9, 16, 19, 65, 66, 99; Saxony, 3
yei, 64, 101. *See also* pictorial designs

zigzags, 2, 4, 15, 69, 70, 92. *See also* geometric designs